My Life with
DIABETES

Life can be Beautiful even with
Type 1 Diabetes

me

Raphaelle

Raphaelle and Hortense Dossous-Parris

Balboa Press books may be ordered through booksellers or by contacting:

Balboa Press
A Division of Hay House
1663 Liberty Drive
Bloomington, IN 47403
www.balboapress.com.au
1 (877) 407-4847

ISBN: 978-1-5043-1753-5 (sc)
ISBN: 978-1-5043-1754-2 (e)

Print information available on the last page.

Balboa Press rev. date: 04/27/2019

BALBOA.
PRESS
A DIVISION OF HAY HOUSE

INTRODUCTION

You must wonder why I wrote this book, right? Well, at first it was for a competition at school in which I won first prize. Then mum suggested that I share my experience with other kids, those persons who might not feel as confident as I am, to express themselves or understand what is going on in their lives.

When I started writing for the competition my story was different. I was writing about a princess. My mother asked me, "Why are you copying others? You need to be original. What do princesses do? They do nothing but get dressed up and wait for a prince to save them. Is that what you want?"

"No!" I said. My mum told me to write about myself since I am an interesting person. She told me to think about something that is important to me. It took me a few minutes to think about something significantly important in my life. I said "I know what! Let's talk about Diabetes!" My mum was elated, she gave me an exercise book and told me I had work to do.

This book is dedicated to all the boys and girls with diabetes. I hope my story will inspire you in some way. You can do anything. To those of you reading this book but don't have diabetes, I hope this book will bring you to a greater understanding of what those of us who have diabetes go through every day in order to survive and live a happy, healthy life. If you have a friend who has diabetes, please be supportive.

CHAPTER 1

My name is Raphaelle Dossous-Parris and I have Type 1 Diabetes. I started writing this book when I was seven years old. For those of you who do not know about Type 1 Diabetes disease; it occurs when your body produces too little or does not produce any insulin at all.

The organ in your body that produces insulin is called the pancreas; it is a bit difficult to pronounce. The pancreas sits across the back of the abdomen, behind the stomach. It helps to break down carbohydrates, fats and proteins and it keeps the level of chemicals in the body balanced.

Here is a drawing of the pancreas and where is it located in the body.

My mum thinks it is important to know a little bit of the history of diabetes and the origins of the word.

Diabetes Mellitus is derived from the Greek word "diabetes" which means "siphon- to pass through". The word "Mellitus" is a Latin word which means "honeyed or sweet." In diabetics, excess sugar is found in the blood as well as the urine. Diabetes is not new at all because the term "sweet urine" can be found in the ancient Greek, Chinese, Egyptian, Indian and Persian literature.

Insulin allows the body to use the food we eat, which gives it the energy needed to move. Glucose is a sugar that turns into energy. You need energy to do all kinds of things like running, reading and playing. I take insulin to help my body use the food that I eat by turning glucose into energy.

According to the Diabetes Australia website, "Insulin is a hormone made by beta cells in the pancreas. When we eat, insulin is released into the blood stream where it helps your blood sugar level from getting too high or too low. It moves glucose from the food we have eaten into our cells to be used as energy".

How did my diabetes start? I don't remember exactly how it started but I had a cold and a fever for two weeks, my mum said. The cough was dry, no mucus and no stuffy nose. My fever was mostly at night. I was thirsty all the time and was constantly waking up to drink water. I used to feel woozy and see colours in front of my eyes. Here is a picture of me feeling woozy.

One night I woke up in a pool of urine. My pyjamas were wet, and the smell was very strong. My mum changed the sheets and two hours later the whole bed was wet again.

The next day we went to the doctor. He had a worried look on his face and said, "I am afraid the symptoms you described are signs of diabetes". The doctor asked the nurse to bring a kit and he tested my blood sugar. It was at 20.2. He said to my mum, "I would advise you to take her to the hospital immediately, because these numbers are too high". I did not understand anything at all!

The same afternoon, I was in the hospital with a drip in my arm and both my mum and dad had worried looks on their faces. Many doctors and nurses came in and out of the room to talk to my parents. I was feeling fine. I wanted to go to the playground and play more than anything.

In the days that followed, lots of things changed. We went to the Diabetes Centre, we saw the doctor and spent lots of time with the dietician. My parents and I learned about carbohydrates, insulin, sugar intake, portion size, how to use the machine to check my blood glucose and how to prick my fingers. My mum said it was overwhelming! My school had to be informed of my diabetes, all the school teachers, my dance teacher as well as my Choi Kwang Do instructor.

Now I must check my blood glucose every time before I eat.

Step 1 prick your finger.

Step 2 open a strip and put it in the glucose monitor.

Step 3 put the blood from your finger on the strip and wait for the reading.

My numbers are recorded in a book that the doctor uses to estimate my average. At first, I was scared to prick my finger but then I was alright. The doctor said if you go too high like 20 or 30 you can go into a coma and die.

If your numbers are past 50, they are off the chart, you will pass out, go into a coma or have something called Ketoacidosis. This part is very important!

Here is an illustration of a working pancreas and a non-working pancreas.

Working Pancreas

Insulin-Food-Energy

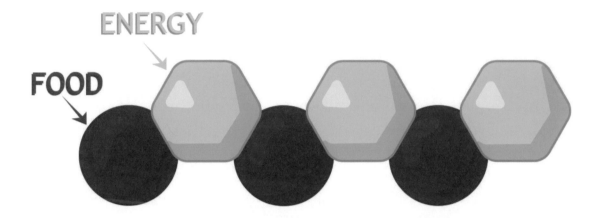

Pancreas not working

Food-NO insulin-No Energy

Ketoacidosis

According to the Science of Diabetes Organization, Ketoacidosis is a serious condition associated with illness or very high blood glucose levels in Type 1 Diabetes. It is a sign of insufficient insulin. Without enough insulin, the body's cells cannot use glucose for energy. When that happens, the body starts to burn fat for energy instead. This leads to the accumulation of a dangerous chemical substance in the body called Ketones, which appears in the urine.

I had that once. I had a stomach bug and I was unable to eat because I was vomiting, and I had diarrhoea. I could not stand the smell of food; my blood sugar was rising although I had not eaten anything, so my mum decided to take me to the hospital. I was put on a drip in order to rehydrate me and two days later when my sugar stabilised, I went back home.

I will tell you about my health

I don't eat any lollies or sweets anymore; they are not good for me. If I were to eat one lolly it would make my blood sugar so high, it could make me sick.

When my blood sugar is high, I feel thirsty, my heart starts beating fast, my saliva becomes foamy and fills my mouth. I don't have as much energy as I normally do. I get cranky and teary.

When I am low my heart starts racing in my body and I feel weak all over, my legs can barely hold me. My vision becomes blurred, my fingers twitch and I feel like I am going to faint.

I eat very healthy now! Sometimes I get a green drink in the morning. I eat lots of green vegetables and not too much rice, but I love rice. My mum makes brown rice with lots of vegetables for me. It is yummy! I can eat fish and meat; duck is my favourite. My mum is a chef at making duck and dad is good at cooking fish. My plate looks like this:

Things I can eat: strawberries, blueberries, blackberries, wild berries, oranges and one quarter of an apple. Lots of greens, brown rice, plantain, sweet potatoes, seaweed, lettuce, lots of cucumbers, celery, capsicum, fish, meat, duck, broccoli, cabbage, cauliflower, black beans and lentils.

Things I don't eat lollies, cakes, sweets, white rice, carrots, beets, regular sugar and processed meat.

I don't eat frozen foods from the supermarket because they are sometimes full of sugar and things that we are not sure are good for me. My mum makes bread for me and she does not add sugar and "all the other ingredients that we can't even pronounce", she says. I eat small snacks like nuts to keep me healthy while I am having fun.

I use different sugar now called Stevia. It is green and it is basically the plant leaves. We are trying to grow it in our garden.

I drink almond milk that mum makes and eat almond butter that she makes too. I love salads and can eat a big bowl.

Here is my bowl of salad.

The doctor said that I am healthy and that I can do all the things I used to do. Diabetes does not stop me from doing anything at all except that we have to plan everything. The year I was diagnosed with diabetes, I came second in my school cross country race and second in swimming. My mum was so proud of me! She always says, 'Believe in yourself!'

I dance ballet, tap and jazz, I have been dancing since I was 3 years old.

My dream is to be one of the lead dancers in The Alvin Ailey American Dance Theatre in New York.

I also do martial arts, to be precise, Choi Kwang Do with my mum and my brother. I am a yellow belt senior.

I ride my bike to school most mornings. I also ride my scooter with my mum and my brother. We ride for fun on some afternoons. I swim 3 days a week and I love drawing. I have not missed any school days due to diabetes. We follow a very healthy diet and that has helped me to stay healthy. I go to school, follow my school rules and work keenly at my studies like any other student.

Here are some of my paintings.

Sometimes I think it is unfair that I can't eat certain things, but I have a mum that can find substitutes and make or bake anything. I am happy eating my vegetables; they make me strong and healthy. I did not eat junk food before, so I am not missing it. All my family members had to change their diet because of me.

My mum says it is better that way. My dad is doing a lot of research on diabetes, looking at what is the best diet to follow. I have learnt lots of new words like carbohydrates, insulin, low GI, glucose, pancreas etc.

This is my life with diabetes. It has been many years and I am still healthy.

I am happy to be me.

Words learned: Diabetes Type 1, Autoimmune disease, pancreas, insulin, Beta cell, enzyme, carbohydrate, ketoacidosis, low GI, glucose, stevia.

Some definitions

Diabetes

Pancreas

Insulin

Beta cell

Carbohydrate

Ketoacidosis

Low GI

Glucose

Stevia

ACKNOWLEDGMENTS

I want to thank my mum and dad for encouraging me to write this book. I am not sure where I would be without their encouragement and support. I am especially appreciative of the help, guidance and care that I received from my doctor and nurses at the Diabetes Centre in Cairns. The nutritionist was phenomenal as well as the nurse.

I am extremely grateful to the Diabetes Association of Barbados who cared for me for a year, and still provide me with medication even to this day, through the Sponsor-A-Child with Diabetes Programme. I was also able to participate in one of their World Diabetes Day 5K fun walks with my brother, who ran all the way. I am thankful for my Dad who researches diets and lifestyles for diabetics.

I am extremely grateful to my editor, Pamela Stroude for her thoughtful guidance and kind assistance.

I am deeply thankful to all of those who donated financially through GoFundMe and other means to help this book become a reality.

BIBLIOGRAPHY

Mandal, Dr. Ananya, "History of Diabetes - Origin of the term diabetes", News Medical Life Sciences, https://www.news-medical.net/health/History-of-Diabetes.aspx

Diabetes Australia, "Insulin",

https://www.diabetesaustralia.com.au/insulin

Printed in the United States
By Bookmasters